Circus ponies

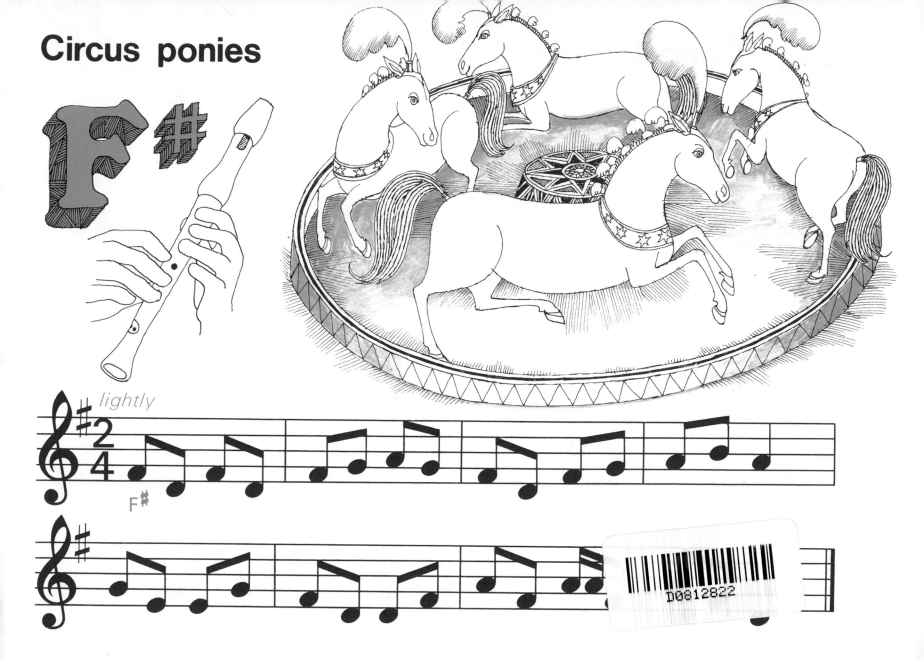

1

Flying trapeze

with a steady swing

F♯

2

Pipe and drum

Old Wardour castle

proudly

Monkey rides a bicycle

Street games

The Ringmaster

Dashing round the bonfire

with excitement

Pirates bold

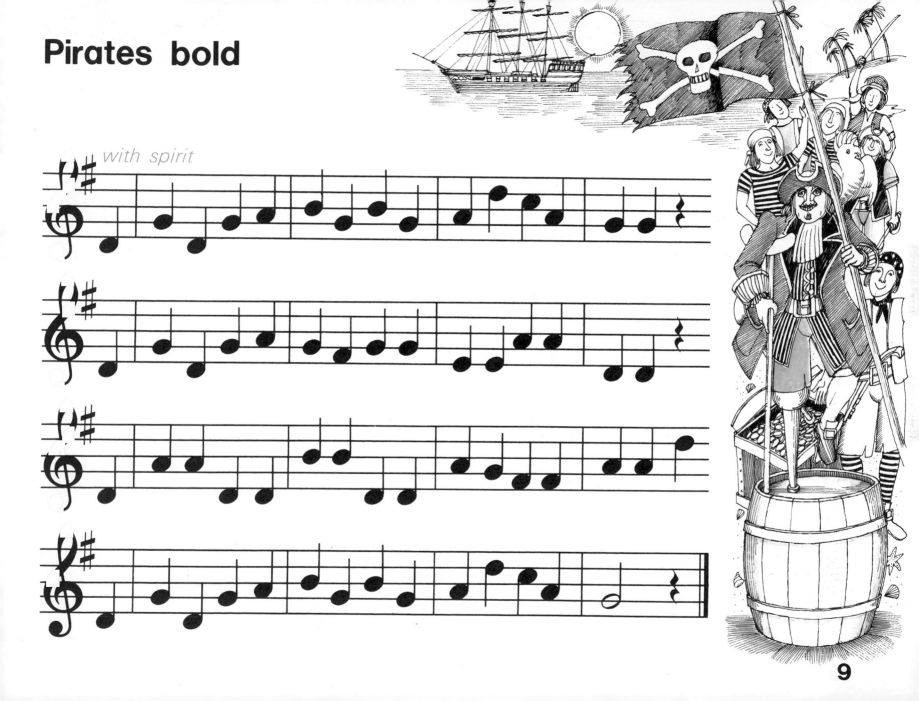

Bareback rider

Indian dancers

slow and sinuous

quick and with strong rhythm

now play the first tune again

11

Sailor's hornpipe

Irish jig

Scottish reel

quickly and neatly

14

Performing seals

Early morning

In the meadow

Hampstead Heath

Seahorses

Lazy Daisy

Sherwood Forest

smoothly

Jugglers

neatly

F♯

F♮

22

Acrobats

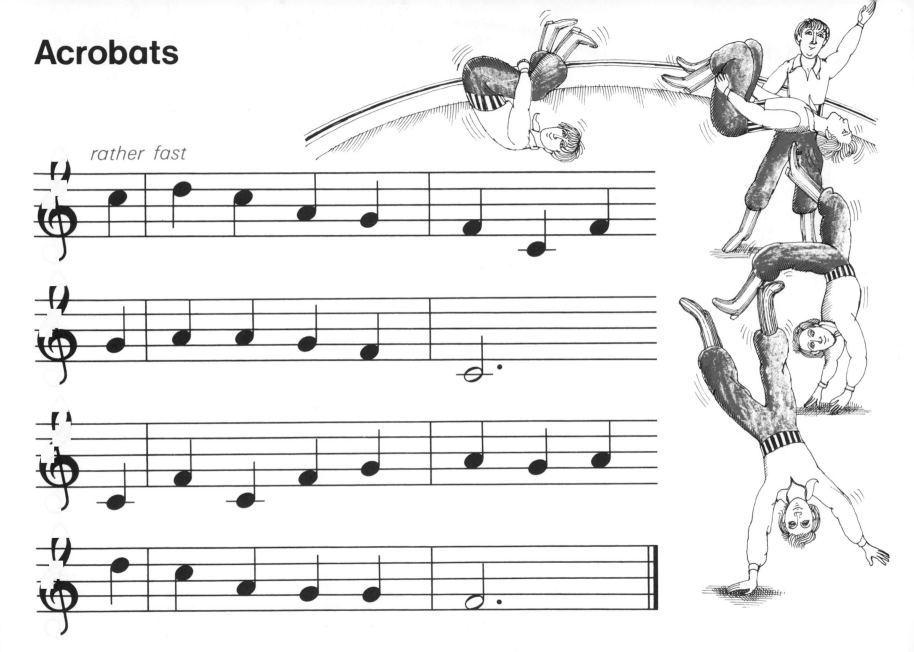

rather fast

Swans

gliding

24

Goodnight

peacefully

B♭

Tightrope walker

Rodeo

lazily

Finish

now play the first part of the tune again

27

The high hills

The old haycart

bumbling

29

Swinging on the gate

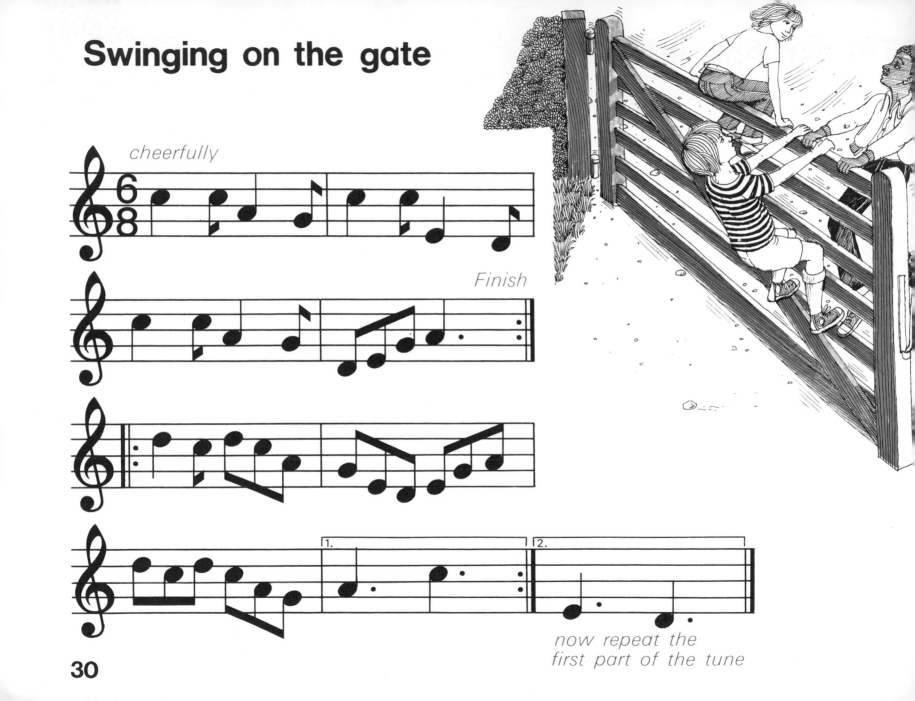

The Gypsy's baby

Whistling boy

cheerfully